JOKES
for
GIRLS

JOKES FOR GIRLS

Summersdale Publishers Ltd
46 West Street
Chichester
West Sussex
PO19 1RP
UK

www.summersdale.com

Printed and bound in the Czech Republic

ISBN: 978-1-84953-473-4

Substantial discounts on bulk quantities of Summersdale books are available to corporations, professional associations and other organisations. For details contact Nicky Douglas by telephone: +44 (0) 1243 756902, fax: +44 (0) 1243 786300 or email: nicky@summersdale.com.

JOKES for GIRLS

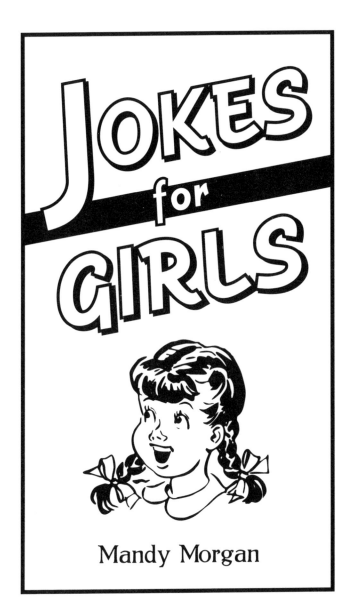

Mandy Morgan

summersdale

Contents

GEOGRAPHICAL GIGGLES

What did the ground say
to the earthquake?

You crack me up.

What has five eyes and is made of water?

The Mississippi River.

What is the smartest American state?

Alabama – it has four As and one B.

Teacher: Where is the English Channel?

Student: I don't know, my
TV doesn't pick it up.

What is the fastest country in the world?

Rush–a.

Teacher: What can you tell me
about the Dead Sea?

Student: I didn't even know it was sick.

Teacher: Where in England is Felixstowe?

Pupil: On the end of Felix's foot.

Why didn't the map grids go to the disco?

Because they were all squares.

What did the sea say to the shore?

Nothing, it just waved.

What city always cheats at exams?

Peking.

What sort of pudding roams
wild in the Arctic Circle?

Moose.

Where do fish keep their money?

In riverbanks.

Why were the rocks excited to
go to the birthday party?

They knew they'd have a
smashing good time.

Funny Felines

What happened to the cat
that ate a ball of wool?

She had mittens.

What do cat actors say on stage?

Tabby or not tabby.

What did the cat say when
he lost all his money?

I'm paw.

What do you do with a blue Burmese?

Try and cheer it up a bit.

How is cat food sold?

Usually purr can.

What is a cat's favourite cereal?
Shredded Tweet.

Why did the cat join the Red Cross?
Because it wanted to be a first-aid kit.

Who was the most powerful cat in China?
Chairman Miaow.

What is cleverer than a talking cat?
A spelling bee.

What is white, sugary, has whiskers
and floats on the sea?

A catameringue.

What is a crazy marmalade
cat's favourite biscuit?

A ginger nut.

Why do cats chase birds?

For a lark.

Where do cats get their information?

Mewspapers.

What happened when the cat
swallowed a coin?

There was some money in the kitty.

What works in a circus, walks a
tightrope and has claws?

An acrocat.

Why did the cat eat some cheese?

So he could wait by the mouse
hole with baited breath.

STAR-CROSSED LAUGHTER

Boy: Haven't I seen you someplace before?

Girl: Yeah, that's why I don't go there anymore.

Boy: Is this seat empty?

Girl: Yes, and this one will be too if you sit down.

Boy: Your place or mine?

Girl: Both. You go to yours and I'll go to mine.

Boy: I'd like to call you. What's your number?

Girl: It's in the phone book.

Boy: But I don't know your name.

Girl: That's in the phone book too.

Boy: I know how to make you smile.

Girl: Then please leave me alone.

Boy: I can tell that you want me.

Girl: Oh, you're so right. I want you... to leave.

Boy: May I see you pretty soon?

Girl: Why? Don't you think I'm pretty now?

Boy: May I hold your hand?

Girl: No thanks, it isn't heavy.

Girl: If we become engaged
will you give me a ring?

Boy: Sure, what's your phone number?

Boy: I love you and I could die for you!

Girl: How soon?

Boy: I would go to the end
of the world for you!

Girl: Yes, but would you stay there?

Boy: Girls whisper they love me.

Girl: Well, they wouldn't admit
it out loud, would they?

WHAT DO YOU GET IF YOU CROSS...

What do you get if you cross
a fridge with a stereo?

Cool music.

What do you get if you cross
a lemon with a cat?

A sourpuss.

What do you get if you cross
an abbot with a trout?

Monkfish.

What do you get if you cross
a zebra with a needle?

Pinstripes.

What do you get if you cross
an elephant with a rhino?

El-if-i-no.

What do you get if you cross
a bell with a chicken?

An alarm cluck.

What do you get if you cross
a dog with a rose?

A collie-flower.

What do you get if you cross
a cow with a camel?

Lumpy milkshakes.

What do you get if you cross
a snake with a Lego set?

A boa constructor.

What do you get if you cross a computer with a potato?

Microchips.

What do you get if you cross an aerobics class with apple pie?

Puff pastry.

What do you get if you cross a teacher with a vampire?

Blood tests.

What do you get if you cross a hare with the bagpipes?

Hopscotch.

What do you get if you cross
a cow with a mule?

Milk with a kick to it.

What do you get if you cross a
motorway with a skateboard?

Run over.

What do you get if you cross
a teddy bear with a pig?

A teddy boar.

What do you get if you cross
a skunk with an owl?

A smelly bird that doesn't give a hoot.

What do you get if you cross
a frog with some mist?

Kermit the Fog.

What do you get if you cross
a kangaroo with a mink?

A fur coat with pockets.

What do you get if you cross a
tomcat with a Pekingese?

A Peking tom.

What do you get if you cross a
grizzly bear with a harp?

A bear-faced lyre.

What do you get if you cross
a pineapple with a zipper?

A fruit fly.

What do you get if you cross an
orange with a comedian?

Peels of laughter.

What do you get if you cross an
elephant with a kangaroo?

Big holes all over Australia.

What do you get if you cross
a dog with a telephone?

A golden receiver.

IT'S A BEAUTIFUL WORLD

How do hairstylists
speed up their job?

They take short cuts.

What do you get if you cross a hairdresser and a bucket of cement?

Permanent waves.

What do you get if you cross a wireless with a hairdresser?

Radio waves.

I almost got my haircut, but I thought I'd mullet over first.

Teacher: I see you don't cut your hair any longer.

Pupil: No sir, I cut it shorter.

What do cavemen use to clean their teeth?

Dental moss.

Mother always uses lemon to clear
her complexion. Maybe that's
why she looks so sour.

Why did the woman put
lipstick on her forehead?

She was trying to make up her mind.

People who get complimented on their
hair usually let it go to their head.

Where do make-up artists park their cars?

Compact spaces.

Why are beauticians better
at resolving fights?

Because they know how to make-up.

Why is it harder for women to whistle?

Because their lipstick.

Who won the skeleton beauty contest?

No body.

Two silk worms had a race.

They ended up in a tie.

What do you call shoes made from bananas?

Slippers.

Did you hear about those
new reversible jackets?

I'm excited to see how they turn out.

Knock knock.
Who's there?
Lucy.
Lucy who?
Lucy Lastic makes your pants fall down.

Why did the golfer have an
extra pair of pants?

In case he got a hole in one.

Why do bears have fur coats?

Because they'd look silly wearing jackets.

What do penguins wear on their heads?

Ice caps.

What kind of ties do pigs wear?

Pig's ties.

Why don't you wear a cardboard belt?

That would be a waist of paper.

What kind of socks does a pirate wear?

Arrrrrgyle.

Why did the clown wear loud socks?

So his feet wouldn't fall asleep.

What did the shoes say to the hat?

You go on a head, I'll follow you on foot.

Why did the leopard wear a striped shirt?

So she wouldn't be spotted.

What do you call a dinosaur
wearing a cowboy hat?

Tyrannosaurus Tex.

What does a cloud wear under her raincoat?

Thunderwear.

Who makes the best prehistoric
reptile clothes?

A dino-sewer.

What do you call doing 2,000
pounds of laundry?

Washing-ton.

Where do frogs leave their hats and coats?

In the croakroom.

A man walked into a shoe shop and tried on a pair of shoes. 'How do they feel?' asked the sales assistant. 'A bit tight,' the man replied. The assistant bent down to check the shoes and said, 'Try pulling the tongue out.' 'They thtill feel a bith tighth,' answered the man.

Did you hear about the man who put on a pair of clean socks every day?

By the end of the week he couldn't get his shoes on.

A man walked into an army store and asked if they had any camouflage trousers. 'Yes, we have,' replied the assistant, 'but we can't find them!'

A little boy puts his shoes on by himself, but his mother notices he's got them mixed up. 'Sweetie,' she says, 'you've put your shoes on the wrong feet.' The little boy looks at her and says, 'But these are the only feet I've got!'

What kind of shoes do all spies wear?

Sneakers.

An Elephant Never Forgets

What goes up slowly and comes down quickly?

An elephant in a lift.

Why were the elephants thrown
out of the swimming pool?

Because they couldn't hold their trunks up.

What did the grape say when
the elephant stood on it?

Nothing, it just let out a little wine.

Have you heard about the elephant
that went on a crash diet?

He ran into three cars, a bus
and two fire engines.

Why do elephants do well in school?

Because they have a lot of grey matter.

What did the baby elephant get when
the daddy elephant sneezed?

Out of the way.

Why do elephants have short tails?

Because they can't remember long stories.

Why do elephants have trunks?

Because they'd look pretty
stupid with suitcases.

What's the definition of hope?

An elephant hanging over a cliff
with its tail tied to a daisy.

Study Hard, Laugh Harder

Teacher: Do you have trouble making decisions?

Pupil: Well... yes and no.

Pupil: Sir, my dog ate my homework.

Teacher: And where's your dog now?

Pupil: He's at the vet's – he doesn't like maths either.

Why did the primary school teacher marry the caretaker?

He swept her off her feet.

Pupil: I don't think I deserved zero for this exam.

Teacher: Me neither. But I couldn't give you any lower.

Teachers who take class attendance
are absent-minded.

Teacher: You know you can't
sleep in my class.

Pupil: I know. But maybe if you
were just a little quieter, I could.

What do you call a teacher without students?

Happy.

Teacher: Why have you got cotton wool in your ears, do you have an infection?

Pupil: Well you keep saying that things go in one ear and out the other, so I am trying to keep them all in.

Amy was describing her teacher to her mum and called her 'mean but fair'. 'Just what do you mean by that?' her mother asked. 'She is mean to everybody,' Amy replied.

The little boy wasn't getting good marks in school. One day he surprised the teacher and said, 'I don't want to scare you, but my daddy says if I don't get better grades, somebody is going to get a spanking.'

Teacher: You copied from Simon's exam paper didn't you?

Pupil: How did you know?

Teacher: Simon's paper says, 'I don't know' and you have put 'Me, neither'.

Pupil (on phone): My son has a bad cold and won't be able to come to school today.

School Secretary: Who is this?

Pupil: This is my father speaking.

Mother: How do you like your new teacher?

Son: I don't. She told me to sit up the front for the present and then she didn't give me one.

Teacher: You missed school yesterday, didn't you?

Pupil: Not very much.

Why did the student eat his homework?

Because the teacher said it
was a piece of cake.

'Johnny, where's your homework?' Miss
Martin said sternly to her most troublesome
pupil. 'My dog ate it,' he responded.
'Johnny, I've been a teacher for sixteen
years. Do you really expect me to believe
that?' 'It's true, Miss Martin, I swear it is,'
insisted Johnny. 'I had to smear it with
honey, but I finally got him to eat it.'

Teacher: How can you make so many mistakes in just one day?

Pupil: I get up early.

Teacher: I told you to stand at the end of the line.

Pupil: I tried, but there was someone already there.

Teacher: You aren't paying attention to me. Are you having trouble hearing?

Pupil: No, miss, I'm having trouble listening!

Son: Hey, Dad! I've got some great news for you!

Father: What, son?

Son: Remember that £100 you promised me if I got good grades?

Father: I certainly do.

Son: Well, you get to keep it.

Teacher: Why can't you ever answer any of my questions?

Pupil: Well, if I could there wouldn't be much point in me being here.

Father: How do you like going to school?

Son: The going bit is fine, as is the coming home bit, but I'm not too keen on the time in between.

Teacher: Why were you late?

Student: Sorry, sir, I overslept.

Teacher: You mean you need to sleep at home too?!

Pupil: Miss, is there life after death?

Teacher: Why do you ask?

Pupil: I may need the extra time to finish all this homework you gave us.

What school do you greet people in?

Hi School.

Daughter: Great news, teacher says we have a test today come rain or shine.

Mum: So what's so great about that?

Daughter: It's snowing outside!

First student: How old is Mr Smith?

Second student: Pretty old. They say he used to teach Shakespeare.

WITTY WAITER

Waiter, why is there a
fly in my wine?

You asked for a red with
a little body in it.

Waiter, this coffee tastes like mud!

Well, it was ground only an hour ago.

Waiter, there are two flies in my soup!

That's OK, the extra one is on the house.

Waiter, what's this spider doing in my soup?

Why sir, it looks like it's learning to swim.

Waiter, there is a small slug in this lettuce.

I'm sorry, madam, would you like
me to fetch you a bigger one?

Waiter, my lunch is talking to me!

Yes, you ordered today's special
– tongue sandwich.

Waiter, there is a slug in my sandwich!

Shhh, or everyone will want one.

Waiter, there is a spider in my bowl; I
demand to speak to the manager.

That's no good, madam, he's
scared of them too.

Waiter, why on earth is there a
dead fly in my burger?

I don't know, sir, perhaps it died after tasting it.

Waiter, watch out! Your thumb's in my soup!

Don't worry, sir, it's not that hot!

Waiter, what's this spider doing
in my alphabet soup!

Probably learning to read, sir.

Waiter, there is a dead fly in my chilli!

Yes, sir, it's the heat that kills them.

Waiter, will my hamburger be long?

No, sir, it will be round.

Waiter, why is there a fly in my ice cream?

Perhaps he likes winter sports.

Waiter, there is a fly in the butter!

Yes sir, it's a butterfly.

Waiter, do you have frogs' legs?

How dare you! This is just how I walk.

Farmyard Fun

What do cows do for fun?

They go to the mooooovies.

What do you give a sick pig?

Oinkment.

Where can you find a horse with no legs?

Where you left it.

Why did the pig go to Vegas?

To play the slop machines.

How long do chickens work?

Around the cluck.

Why don't chickens like people?

They beat eggs.

What do chickens grow on?

Eggplants.

Why are chickens always chatting?

Because talk is cheep.

What did the well-mannered
sheep say at the field gate?

After ewe.

Where did the sheep go on holiday?

The baaaahamas.

Why did the calf miss school?

Because his parents were mooving.

How do cows cut the grass?

With a lawn-mooer.

How do you fit more pigs on your farm?

Build a sty-scraper.

What game do cows play at parties?

Moosical chairs.

Why do cows wear bells?

Because their horns don't work.

What do you call a cow who
lives in an igloo?

An Eskimoo.

What do drunk hens lay?

Scotch eggs.

What do you give a pony with a cold?

Cough stirrup.

Why did the bull rush?

Because it saw the cow slip.

Knock Knock.
Who's there?
The interrupting cow.
The interrupt...
MOOO!

BIRTHDAY BELTERS

What did the big birthday
candle say to the little candle?

You're too young to go out.

What has wings, a long tail
and wears a bow?

A birthday pheasant.

What did the jelly say to the
miserable birthday cake?

What's eating you?

What's a rabbit's favourite party game?

Musical hares.

What's the best thing to buy an
angry rhino for its birthday?

I'm not sure, but for your
sake I hope it likes it.

Why do people put candles
on the top of cakes?

Because you can't really put
them on the bottom.

What kind of birthday cake
is hard as a rock?

Marble cake.

What do snails do on their birthdays?

They shellebrate.

Where's the best place to look
for a present for your cat?

In a catalogue.

What did one candle say to the other?

Don't birthdays burn you up?

Why didn't cavemen send birthday cards?

They could never get the stamps
to stick to the rocks.

What Do You Call...

What do you call a lion wearing a cravat and a flower in its mane?

A dandy lion.

What do you call a cement-eating chicken?

A bricklayer.

What do you call a rabbit with fleas?

Bugs bunny.

What do you call a man with
a spade on his head?

Doug.

What do you call a man without
a spade on his head?

Douglas.

What do you call a man with
a satnav on his head?

Miles.

What do you call a man with
a flat tyre on his head?

Jack.

What do you call a man with a
number plate on his head?

Reg.

What do you call an ant with
five pairs of eyes?

Ant-ten-eye.

What do you call a man with
a toilet on his head?

Lou.

What do you call a woman with
two toilets on her head?

Lulu.

What do you call an elephant that flies?

A jumbo jet.

What do you call a woman with
a radiator on her head?

Anita.

What do you call a woman
with thatch on her head?

Ruth.

What do you call a man with a
plastic bag on his head?

Russell.

What do you call a snake that
gets you into trouble?

A grass snake.

What do you call a man who's
been scratched by your cat?

Claude.

What do you call a man with
a seagull on his head?

Cliff.

What do you call a girl with
a frog on her head?

Lily.

What do you call a girl who keeps
getting hit by footballs?

Annette.

What do you call a snake that
works for the government?

A civil serpent.

What do you call a woman
with a snail on her back?

Shelley.

What do you call a man with a
rucksack covered in salt and pepper?

A seasoned traveller.

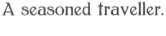

What do you call a cat that's
swallowed a duck?

A duck-filled fatty puss.

What do you call a row of rabbits
running away from you?

A receding hare-line.

What do you call a 100-year-old ant?

An antique.

What do you call two banana skins?

A pair of slippers.

What do you call a blind dinosaur?

Do-you-think-he-saurus.

What do you call a girl with
burgers cooking on her head?

Barbie.

What do you call a litter of dogs that
have just come in from the snow?

Slush puppies.

What do you call a man covered in meat,
sliced carrots and a thick gravy?

Stu.

What do you call a guard with 100 legs?

A sentrypede.

What do you call a sweater that's
jumping up and down?

A bungee jumper.

What do you call a woman with
a strong wind on her head?

Gail.

What do you call a man with a
prayer mat on his head?

Neil.

What do you call a sleeping male cow?

A bull dozer.

Stomach Fillers

What did the nut say
when he sneezed?

Cashew!

What's orange, long and sounds like a parrot?

A carrot.

Why was the soup so expensive?

Because there were twenty-four carrots in it.

Why did the bun whistle?

Because he saw the hot dog.

What did the big tomato say
to his little brother?

Ketchup.

Why did the sales assistant get
fired from the hot dog stand?

For putting her hair in a bun.

What did the salt say to the
melodramatic fry-up?

Stop eggs-aggerating.

What did the photographer
say to the curdled milk?

Say, 'Cheese!'

What's white, round and can't stop giggling?

A tickled onion.

What's the worst vegetable to find on a boat?

A leek.

What's white, sugary and
swings through the trees?

A meringue-utan.

It was an emotional wedding.
Even the cake was in tiers.

What jumps from cake to cake
and tastes like almonds?

Tarzipan.

Why wasn't the bacon allowed to compete in the swimming competition?

It was a sausage meet.

What kind of biscuit can take you to an exotic location?

A plain biscuit.

Why did the raspberries cry?

Because they were in a jam.

Why did the police come round for breakfast?

Because someone had poached the eggs.

Did you hear about the guy who got hit in the head with a can of lemonade?

He was lucky it was a soft drink.

I decided that becoming a vegetarian was a missed steak.

Dad: Now, Sam, tell me frankly do you say prayers before eating?

Son: No Dad, I don't have to, Mum is a good cook.

Two peanuts walk into a bar.

One was a salted.

What do you get when you have
baked beans and onions together?

Tear gas.

What do you get if you cross an
Italian restaurant and a ghost?

Spookhetti!

What do you get if you cross a
hot drink and the universe?

Gravi-tea!

What's the difference between
bogeys and broccoli?

Children won't eat broccoli.

What did the mother ghost tell the
baby ghost when he ate too fast?

Stop goblin your food.

Why couldn't the sesame seed
leave the gambling casino?

Because he was on a roll.

MUSIC MADNESS

Why did the music
teacher need a ladder?

To reach the high notes.

The guitarist passed out on stage, he must have rocked himself to sleep.

Where do the pianists go for vacation?

Florida Keys.

Child: My music teacher said my singing was out of this world.

Mum: Really?

Child: Well, she said it was 'unearthly'.

What musical key do cows sing in?

Beef flat.

How do you clean a tuba?

With a tuba toothpaste.

You're a natural musician. Your tongue
is sharp and your head is flat.

Two drums and a cymbal fall off a cliff!

BADOOM TISH!

Why couldn't the athlete listen to her music?

Because she broke the record.

Why did the music students get into trouble?

They were passing notes.

Why did the fish make such
a good musician?

He knew his scales.

What instruments do trees play?

Woodwinds.

Why couldn't the singer get in the house?

She had the wrong key.

Where did the composer write music?

In a notebook.

Did you hear about the pianist who kept banging his head against the keys?

He was playing by ear.

What do you call a fish musician?

A piano tuna.

Why was the piano player arrested?

Because he got into treble.

What do you get when you drop
a piano down a mine shaft?

A flat minor.

What do you get when you drop
a piano on an army base?

A flat major.

Why did Mozart kill his chickens?

Because they always ran around
clucking, 'Bach! Bach! Bach!'

What type of music are balloons scared of?

Pop music.

What makes music on your head?

A head band.

What has forty feet and sings?

The school choir.

What is the musical part of a snake?

The scales.

What do you call a cow that can play a musical instrument?

A moo-sician.

What part of the turkey is musical?

The drumstick.

What makes pirates such good singers?

They can hit the high Cs.

Knock knock!
Who's there?
Little old lady?
Little old lady who?
I didn't know you could yodel!

Bee-ing Bonkers

What goes zzub, zzub?

A bee flying backwards.

Where did Noah keep his bees?

In the ark hives.

What do bees do if they want
to use public transport?

Wait at a buzz stop.

What does a queen bee do when she burps?

She issues a royal pardon.

What do you call a bee who is
having a bad hair day?

A Frisbee.

Who is the most popular
children's author for bees?

Bee-trix Potter.

What did a mother bee say
to her naughty son?

Bee-hive yourself.

Why do bees hum?

Because they've forgotten the words.

What kind of bee drops things?

A fumble bee.

What did the bee say to the flower?

Hello honey.

What did the confused bee say?

To bee or not to bee.

What bee is good for your health?

Vitamin bee.

What kind of bee should speak up?

A mumble bee.

What does a bee get at a burger bar?

A humburger.

What did the spider say to the bee?

Your honey or your life.

Who is a bee's favourite pop group?

The Bee Gees.

Why do bees have sticky hair?

Because of the honey combs.

Where do bees go on holiday?

Stingapore.

Why did the bee start talking poetry?

He was waxing lyrical

Why did the queen bee kick
out all the other bees?

Because they kept droning on.

EVERYBODY TALKS ABOUT THE WEATHER

Did you hear about the cows
that got caught up in a tornado?

It was an udder disaster.

What did one tornado say to the other?

Let's twist again, like we did last summer.

Why did the woman run outside
with her purse open?

Because she heard there would be
some change in the weather.

Which animal should you never
invite to your barbeque?

A reindeer.

What is fowl weather?

When it starts raining chickens and ducks.

How did the girl lose her dad when they were eating ice lollies?

He got caught up in a Twister.

What's the difference between a horse and the weather?

One is reined up and the other rains down.

What's worse than raining cats and dogs?

Hailing taxis.

What do you have to be careful of when it rains cats and dogs?

Not to step in a poodle.

What did one hurricane say
to the other hurricane?

I've got my eye on you.

What did one lightning bolt say
to the other lightning bolt?

You're shocking.

'You never get anything right,' complained the
teacher. 'What job do you think you'll be able
to do when you leave school?' 'Well,' replied
the pupil, 'I want to be a weather forecaster.'

How do sheep stay warm in winter?

Central bleating.

THE BEAUTIFUL, BRINY SEA

Why did the lobster blush?

Because the sea weed.

What's long, slippery and likes to dance?

A conga eel.

What's round, chocolatey and
found in the ocean?

An oyster egg.

Where are whales weighed?

At a whale weigh station.

Why wouldn't you want to fight an octopus?

They're very well armed.

How do you stop a fish from smelling?

Cut its nose off.

Where do shellfish go to borrow money?

To the prawn broker.

Which fish can perform operations?

A sturgeon.

Two birds sitting on a perch, one says
to the other, 'Can you smell fish?'

What happened to the shark that
swallowed a bunch of keys?

He got lockjaw.

Where do little fish go every morning?

To plaice school.

What is the saddest creature in the sea?

The blue whale.

What do you give a fish that
is hard of hearing?

A herring aid.

Which fish comes out at night?

A starfish.

Which fish go to heaven when they die?

Angelfish.

Two fish in a tank, one says to the other,
'Do you know how to drive this?'

What kind of fish goes well with ice cream?

Jellyfish.

What is a dolphin's favourite TV show?

Whale of Fortune.

Who held the baby octopus to ransom?

Squidnappers.

What was the Tsar of Russia's favourite fish?

Tsardines.

How do fish get to school?

By octobus.

What fish do road workers use?

Pneumatic krill.

Why shouldn't little fish go
out alone at night?

In case they bump into Jack the Kipper.

What did the boy fish say to his girlfriend?

Your plaice or mine?

Where does seaweed look for work?

In the 'kelp wanted' ads.

One kipper says to another, 'Smoking is bad for you.' The other replies, 'Don't worry, I've been cured.'

What kind of fish is useful in freezing weather?

Skate.

What is the best way to communicate with a fish?

Drop it a line.

Why are pirates called pirates?

Because they arrrrrr.

Anyone FOR Tennis?

Why couldn't the man
light the fire?

He was trying to use
a tennis match.

What do you serve but not eat?

A tennis ball.

Why should you never fall in
love with a tennis player?

'Love' means nothing to them.

Why aren't fish good at tennis?

They don't like getting close to the net.

Why is tennis such a noisy sport?

Because the players all raise a racket.

Where do ghosts play tennis?

On a tennis corpse.

Which US state is famous for tennis?

Tennis-see.

What do you call an intelligent tennis player?

A racket scientist.

What do you get if you cross a skunk
and a pair of tennis rackets?

Ping pong.

What time does Sean Connery get
up to play his favourite sport?

Tennish.

THEIR IS ALOT OF KOOL JOKES 'ERE

Teacher: Can someone give me a sentence using the word 'Archaic'?

Pupil: We can't have archaic and eat it too.

'The teacher said I must learn to write more legibly,' the child told his mother. 'But if I do, she'll find out that I can't spell.'

'An abstract noun,' the teacher said, 'is something you can think of, but you can't touch. Can you give me an example of one?' 'Sure,' a teenage boy replied. 'My father's new car.'

Teacher: Now, you must not say, 'I ain't goin'.'
You should say, 'I am not going; he is not
going; we are not going; they are not going.'

Student: Wow! Ain't nobody goin' then?

It's always I before E. Isn't that weird?

Teacher: Which two days of the
week start with the letter 'T'?

Pupil: Today and tomorrow.

Teacher: Conjugate the verb 'to walk' in the simple present tense.

Student: I walk... um... You walk...

Teacher: Quicker, please.

Student: I jog... You jog...

Teacher: Can anyone use the word 'fascinate' in a sentence?

Pupil: My dad bought a new shirt with nine buttons, but he's so fat he was only able to fasten eight.

Teacher: What is the longest word
in the English language?

Pupil: Smiles – because there's a whole
mile between the first and last letter.

What is grammar?

The difference between knowing your
stuff and knowing you're stuff.

A boy answers the phone. The caller
asks, 'Where are your parents?' 'They
ain't here,' the boy replies. 'Come on,
son. Where's your grammar?' says
the caller, shocked. 'My gramma ain't
here neither. She's gone to church!'

A prisoner's favourite punctuation mark is the full stop. It marks the end of his sentence.

A rule of grammar: double negatives are a no-no.

What kind of word would you invite to a fancy tea party?

A proper noun.

Teacher: Can someone give me
a sentence starting with I?

Student: I is–

Teacher: No. Always say, 'I am.'

Student: All right, if you say so. I am
the ninth letter of the alphabet.

Teacher: Spell 'rain'.

Pupil: R–A–N–E.

Teacher: That's the worst spell of rain
we've had around here in a long time!

The teacher asked for sentences using
the word 'beans.' 'My father grows beans,'
said a girl. 'My mother cooks beans,'
said a boy. Then a third child spoke
up, 'We're all human beans,' he said.

Teacher: Describe a synonym.

Pupil: A word you use when you
can't spell the other word.

Teacher: Name two pronouns.

Pupil: Who, me?

Teacher: Correct!

A schoolteacher asked her primary class to construct sentences with the words defeat, detail and defence. There was a pause before a pupil raised his hand and answered, 'The cow jumped over defence and detail went over defeat.'

If 'can't' is the contradiction for 'cannot' then what is 'don't' short for?

Doughnut.

Teacher: Class, we will only have half a day of school this morning.

Pupils: Hooray!

Teacher: We will have the other half day of school this afternoon!

Tummy- TICKLING Technology

My tablet seems to be broken.
I pressed the 'home' button
but I'm still at school...

Mum: Hey honey, what do 'IDK,
LY and TTYL' mean?

Daughter: I don't know, love
you, talk to you later.
Mum: Ok, I'll ask someone else.

How does a computer tell you
it needs more memory?

It says 'byte me'.

Computers are like air conditioners. They
work fine until you start opening windows.

What kind of phones do prisoners use?

Cell phones.

Why did the computer squeak?

Someone stepped on its mouse.

What happened when the monster
ate the electric company?

He was in shock for a week.

What do you get if you cross
a telephone with an iron?

A smooth operator.

What do you call a large person who phones
people, pretending to be somebody else?

A big phone-y.

Why didn't the skeleton need a telephone?

He had no body to talk with.

What do you get if you cross a
phone with a pair of glasses?

A television.

What do you get if you cross a phone
with a birthday celebration?

A party line.

Why didn't the mummy want a telephone?

He always got too wrapped up in his calls.

Acknowledgements

Thanks to Summersdale's Facebook and Twitter friends who sent in their jokes to be included in the book. They are:

Gillian Petley–Jones
Danny Bailey
Phil Shaw
Frankie James
David Rayner

If you're interested in finding out more about our books, find us on Facebook at Summersdale Publishers and follow us on Twitter at @Summersdale.

www.summersdale.com